AF279588

TASTE AND TRADITIONS

Yaiza A. Bermejo Martín

TASTE AND TRADITIONS

ISBN: 978-84-10436-11-4
Depósito Legal: MU 1152-2024

Edición a cargo de: Diego Marín Librero–Editor. S.L.
Merced, 25.30001–Murcia
Tfno. 968 24 28 29 / 968 23 75 78

Introduction

As in any tradition, celebrations in the English speaking countries' culture come hand in hand with food and drink. This is the reason why this book goes through the main festivities, along with texts, questions, videos, recipes and other interesting activities connected with the world of the catering industry.

The aim of this book is to make catering students get familiar with the culture of the language they are learning in A2 English level.

Acknowledgements

Thank you to Charo M. U., who encouraged me to write this book about English food and culture for her catering students, and who involved me in the teaching of foreign languages from a very young age.

Index

🎃🧛‍♂️*HALLOWEEN*🧟‍♂️👽

TASK 1: Do you know what a pumpkin spice latte (PSL) is?

https://www.youtube.com/watch?v=_YgfYwaqZPY

TASK 2:

October 31st is Halloween, the day before All Saints Day. This festival comes from the Celts when they arrived and invaded the British Isles. The word means and people used to say ¨All Hallows' Eve", the night of all Hallows and with time it became Hallowee'en. A time to wear ugly and scary costumes and to light bonfires and candles ¨Jack-O'-Lanterns¨ to frighten away death, evil spirits and bad luck.

Today people celebrate it for fun, and wear costumes not only as ghosts, monsters, skeletons, witches but also as fairies, pirates or anything they like and go to costume parties or just walk on the street or go to visit friends. Children also knock on their neighbours' doors and say ¨trick or treat¨ to get some sweets and candy. Other symbols related to Halloween are spiders, black cats and pumpkins.

Halloween is celebrated mostly among the English-speaking countries UK, Republic of Ireland, US, Canada, Australia, New zealand but with some differences. In Scotland and the Isle of Man you can see the Celtic tradition celebrating October 31st as the last day of the year in the pagan calendar through Samhain celebrations. In the UK people don't get crazy with Halloween home decorations. Costumes in the US and Canada aren't as scary as costumes in the UK. Trick or treat is less common in the UK than in the US. And in Scotland and Ireland people carve a turnip instead of a pumpkin - the tradition of the pumpkin started in North America with the first pilgrims-.

As in any tradition, food is a fundamental part and plays an important role to gather people. Pumpkin pie, pumpkin bread, pumpkin soup, candy apples, toffee apples, apple bread, caramel corn and almost anything you can prepare with Autumn products are typical at this time of year.

Answer these questions:

1. How many of these traditions are new for you?
2. Do you celebrate Halloween in a similar way?
3. Have you ever made a pumpkin pie? Did you use a recipe?
4. Do you have similar traditions in your country?
5. Is food important in the way Halloween is celebrated?

TASK 3:
Pumpkin pie recipe

750g.pumpkin (canned or homemade)
350g. shortcrust pastry
140g. caster sugar
A pinch of salt
A pinch of grated fresh nutmeg
A pinch of cinnamon

2 eggs beaten

25g. melted butter

175 ml. milk

10gr. Icing sugar

Watch the video:

https://www.bbcgoodfood.com/recipes/pumpkin-pie

Pumpkin soup recipe:

20ml. olive oil

2 chopped onions

1kg. pumpkin (peeled and chopped)

700ml. vegetable stock or chicken stock

150ml. Cream

For the croutons: Wholemeal bread, olive oil and pumpkin seeds

Watch the video:

https://www.bbcgoodfood.com/recipes/pumpkin-soup

With the information in these two videos, fill in the grid below:

INGREDIENTS:	UTENSILS:	PREPARATION VERBS:

Pumpkin bread:

Read the text and fill in the blanks with these words:

Raisins, prepare, bread, baked.

Pumpkin bread is a type of moist quick ________ made with pumpkin. The pumpkin can be cooked and softened before being used or simply ________ with the bread; using canned pumpkin renders it a simpler dish to ________. Additional ingredients include nuts (such as walnuts) and ________. Pumpkin bread. Pumpkin walnut bread.

https://en.wikipedia.org/wiki/Pumpkin_bread#:~:text=Pumpkin%20bread%20is%20a%20type,Pumpkin%20walnut%20bread

Circle the odd one out and write a sentence with each one of the circled words

Ghost   —   Mummy   —Candy apple — Witch

Pumpkin pie — Pumpkin soup - Toffee apple - Carrot

Vampire — Fruit — Jack-o-lantern — Black cat

Barrel — Goblin — Bat — Spider

Bottle — Monster — Broom — Skull

....

....

....

....

....

....

You can also have a look at these videos by the famous American TikToker Kennedy Walsh and name the main ingredients she uses in her recipes.

https://www.tiktok.com/@c4tluvr666/video/7279552380545355051?_r=1&_t=8gkxIJ7q5VR

https://www.tiktok.com/@c4tluvr666/video/7135229252051602734?_r=1&_t=8gkxPQUxZfV

....
....
....
....

Now you can prepare your own and original recipe for Halloween.
GOOD LUCK!!!!

 GUY FAWKES' DAY: BONFIRE NIGHT

TASK 1

Have you ever heard this poem?

Remember Remember the 5th of November - Guy Fawkes Fireworks Night Poem

https://www.youtube.com/watch?v=L7hHL33lQ0I

TASK 2

Bonfire night or Guy Fawkes' Day is celebrated every 5th November in Britain with fireworks, bonfires and burning a "guy" made of old newspapers, straw and old clothes.

But who was Guy Fawkes?

 Guy Fawkes was a Catholic Englishman and tried to kill King James I - who was Protestant and didn't like people with other religious ideas- by blowing up the Houses of Parliament with 36 barrels of gunpowder. It was the year 1605 and Guy Fawkes with 13 Catholic conspirators were preparing the plot when one of them sent a letter to a friend in the Parliament warning him about the 5th November. The letter was given to the King and the conspirators were caught and taken to prison in the Tower of London. They were executed for treason in January 1606. The king was still "well and alive".

Today, 5th November people celebrate it with fireworks displays, children make dummies of Guy Fawkes and ask for money in the streets saying "a penny for the guy" to buy fireworks and, later, burn them. There are also bonfires in the streets where people cook and eat sausages, potatoes, chestnuts and corn. Candy apples or any other autumn fruit or vegetable is also cooked and eaten at this festival.

Choose the right answer:

1- What countries celebrate Guy Fawkes?
    a) United States
    b) Britain
    c) Australia

2- How many conspirators helped Fawkes?
    a) Ten
    b) Thirteen
    c) Thirty

3- When is Bonfire Night celebrated?
   a) 31st October
   b) 6th November
   c) 5th November

4- How many gunpowder barrels were prepared
to blow up the Houses of Parliament?
   a) Twenty-six
   b) Thirteen
   c) Thirty-six

5- What is typically eaten at this festival?
   a) Candy apples,roasted chestnuts and any
      other autumn fruit or vegetable
   b) Sausages and eggs
   c) Fried potatoes

TASK 3

Watch these videos:

The Crazy History Behind Bonfire Night In England | Legendary Locations

How to Make Caramel Apples

https://www.youtube.com/watch?v=YIqS6blTTwk

https://www.youtube.com/watch?v=8nngt2XvvHM

Comment with your classmate and answer these questions:

Have you ever prepared toffee apples?
Have you ever tried them?

24

Do you think the recipe in your country is the same?

Can you think of traditional things to eat at this time of the year?

Can you prepare them? Can you name some of the ingredients?

Think in one of these recipes you like and write it down.

Ingredients:

……………………………………………………….

……………………………………………………….

……………………………………………………….

……………………………………………………….

……………………………………………………….

Recipe:

………………………………………………………………………………………

………………………………………………………………………………………

………………………………………………………………………………………

TASK 4

Watch this TikTok:

https://vm.tiktok.com/ZGebCvMJ7/

This place is found in Yorkshire. Identify
Yorkshire in this map of the UK:

https://www.theedkins.co.uk/jo/maps/uktowns.htm

 REMEMBRANCE DAY

TASK 1

Remembrance Day or Poppy Day was originally called Armistice Day to commemorate the end of World War I which took place on the 11th November 1918. From then on people from the USA, UK, Canada and Australia remember those who died in World War I and World War II the 11th hour on the 11th day of the 11th month wearing a poppy pinned on their clothes and keeping a minute of silence.

The symbol of the poppy for Remembrance Day started with a poem written by a Canadian soldier and surgeon who fought in World War I called John McCrae. The title of the poem is In Flanders Fields and was inspired by the red flowers which grew in the Western battlefield and also in the author's impression of blood and dead bodies after the battle.

The poem was first published on 8th December 1915 and in 1921 the poppy became a symbol of Remembrance Day. Poppies were and are made and sold to raise money for disabled veterans.

TASK 2

Read the poem:

In Flanders fields the poppies blow

Between the crosses, row on row,

That mark our place; and in the sky

The larks, still bravely singing, fly

Scarce heard amid the guns below.

We are the Dead. Short days ago

We lived, felt dawn, saw sunset glow,

Loved and were loved, and now we lie,

In Flanders fields.

Take up our quarrel with the foe:

To you from failing hands we throw

The torch; be yours to hold it high.

If ye break faith with us who die

We shall not sleep, though poppies grow

In Flanders fields.

Then, watch this video

Leonard Cohen recites "In Flanders Fields" by John McCrae | Legion Magazine

And answer these questions

What is the symbol of Remembrance Day?
What do people do at the 11th hour on the 11th
day of the 11th month?
What is the title of the poem which created the
symbol for this celebration?
Do you think it is important to remember what
happened in World War I and II?

THANKSGIVING

Thanksgiving was celebrated for the first time in 1621 in what is now called Massachusetts with Pilgrims and Wampanoag Indians and using products from the land such as corn, potatoes and wild turkey.

In 1863 Abraham Lincoln declared Thanksgiving a national holiday and it was celebrated the last Thursday in November. With President Theodore Roosevelt the celebration in the USA changed to the fourth Thursday in November. In Canada people celebrate it on the second Monday in October.

Nowadays Thanksgiving is a time to be thankful and it is also a time for family and meals. Turkey, smashed potatoes, Indian corn, cranberry gravy, pumpkin pie are some of the typical dishes that are cooked for the occasion.

TASK 1

Underline the odd one out

Pilgrims - Wampanoag - Cook
January- October - November
Pumpkin -   Rice - Corn
Smashed - Stuffing - Fried
1563 - 1621 - 1863
TASK 2

Watch this video to know more about
thanksgiving....

Thanksgiving history and traditions. ESL/ESOL/EFL A1-A2 video

https://www.youtube.com/watch?v=fhgoB3qA_qk

Answer these questions

1. Did you know about all these traditions?

....

2. What was the name of the ship where the Pilgrims sailed?

....

3. What was the name of the continent they left?

....

4. Can you name 3 of the dishes you could see in the video?

....

....

....

TASK 2

Watch this TikTok and name as many foods
(from the video) as you can:

https://vm.tiktok.com/ZGebC7xhE/

....

....

....

....

....

....

....

SAINT ANDREW'S DAY 

TASK 1

St Andrew's Day is the festivity of the Apostle Andrew and is celebrated in Scotland and by Scottish people around the world every year on the 30 November. St Andrew became the patron saint of Scotland in 1320.

St Andrew's Day is celebrated with tasty food and drink, music, ceilidh dancing and parties all day long.

Scotland's food is a fundamental thing on St Andrew's Day. The classical soup is made of smoked haddock, potatoes and onions and it is a common starter followed by the traditional main course haggis served with turnip and mashed potato. The typical Scottish dessert, Clootie dumpling, is a pudding made of dried fruit, breadcrumbs, flour, spices and beef suet and it can be served hot with custard.

To know more about St Andrew's Festival, watch this video:

St Andrew's Day: Explained, a little.

https://www.youtube.com/watch?v=zWaGYgcFYu0

Then, choose the odd one out and say why:

kilt - haggis - clootie dumpling

....

custard - backpipe- ceilidh dancing

....

Fireworks – music - bonfires

....

TASK 2

Do you want to know how to prepare haggis and clootie dumplings ? 🍴 😋
Watch these videos:

https://www.youtube.com/watch?v=DKblUst5sd0

https://www.youtube.com/watch?v=z_zMmEYGj54

List the main ingredients of one of these two recipes

🎄 CHRISTMAS 🎋

TASK 1

How much do you know about Christmas in Britain and in English-speaking countries?

What is the Christmas Advent Calendar?

a) Normal calendar
b) December
c) Calendar which starts the first Sunday before Christmas. Every day you have activities, games, etc.

What do crackers usually have inside?

a) A sentence and a chickpea
b) A crown and a small toy
c) A small present, a paper hat and a joke

What is a Yule Log?

a) A typical Christmas meal
b) A typical Christmas dessert
c) A typical Christmas tree

What is Santa Claus`s favourite food?

   a) White milk and cookies
   b) A piece of cake
   c) Chocolate

What is December 26th?

   a) Christmas Eve
   b) Boxing Day
   c) Christmas Day

TASK 2

Read the text:

At Christmas Christians around the world celebrate the birth of Jesus Christ.

It's a time for family, friends and the people you love and sometimes it involves travelling to your hometown to spend time with your relatives.

Everything starts in Advent, a word that comes from Latin and means arrival. It begins on the fourth Sunday before Christmas. People usually buy Advent calendars to countdown to Christmas Day.

The most famous decoration is the Christmas tree which is a pine tree decorated with balls, tinsels and lights. Some people also put a nativity scene at home.

24 December is Christmas Eve. Groups of singers sing in the streets or go from house to house singing. Children hang stockings on the fireplace

for Father Christmas to fill. It is also time for last minute shopping, food preparation at home for the following day or even for the midnight church service.

25 December is Christmas Day, the day of the birth of Jesus Christ. People open their presents and have a special meal with the family. The typical Christmas dinner consists of roasted turkey, roasted vegetables and potatoes accompanied by pigs in blankets (sausages wrapped in bacon). And the traditional desserts are mince pies (sweet pastry cakes with dried fruit inside), Christmas pudding(dried fruit, candied fruit peel in a dense sponge cake), Yule Logs(cocoa sponge cake filled with cocoa and whipped cream), and Christmas cakes (fruit cake made with pudding). Christmas crackers (coloured paper tubes filled with a paper hat, a toy and a riddle or joke) are also part of the celebration.

26 December is Boxing Day and it is a public holiday in Britain, New Zealand, Australia and Canada. People give money or presents to their

workers, trades people and also to poor people. It is typical to eat sausage rolls to celebrate the traditional post Christmas servants' day off.

Answer these questions about the text:

1. When does Advent begin?

    ....

2. When is the British big meal ?

    ....

3. Name the 3 ingredients that are more often used in British desserts at Christmas

    ....

4. Name 4 things people in the UK do at Christmas

    ....

TASK 3

Watch these videos:

Christmas turkey:

Roast A Turkey With Gordon Ramsay

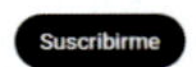
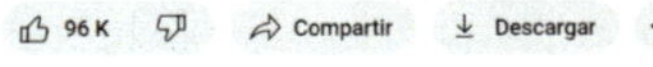

https://www.youtube.com/watch?v=XO5DF8soxwM

Christmas pudding:

https://www.youtube.com/watch?v=3XOKmaElzqw

Mince pies:

https://www.youtube.com/watch?v=WDA60XAW7yo

Which one would you choose to cook it yourself and why?

....

....

....

Match the ingredients with the dish or dishes

Olive oil

Currants

Lemon

Flour   Christmas pudding

Suet   Christmas turkey

Butter   Mince pie

Brandy

Garlic

Onion

TASK 4

Design your own Christmas Eve dinner: What would you make?

✏️

https://vm.tiktok.com/ZGebCXheD/

....

....

....

....

....

....

 AUSTRALIA

TASK 1

Read the text:

Australia is a varied and interesting country with an Indigenous Australian population of around fifty thousand years -oldest culture alive- and more than 250 languages spoken by the year 1788 before European people arrived.

Today, 26 January is Australia National Day and it commemorates the arrival of the First British Fleet in 1788 in Sidney. However there is a lot of controversy with this celebration as lands and culture were taken off from Aboriginal and Torres Strait Islander people at that time.

The Union Jack was used from 1788 to 1901, when the Commonwealth of Australia was created. There was a competition and the winner was as follows: Blue colour flag with the Union Jack on the top left corner. The Commonwealth Star is a seven point big white star placed under the Union

Jack which represents Australian States and territories. And finally, the Southern Cross because you can always see it at night in the Australian sky.

These are the three traditional flags

The Aboriginal Flag, the Australian National Flag and the Torres Strait Islander Flag.

TASK 2

Find or guess the meaning of these symbols:

Sun

Southern Cross   Britain

Red and black colour   Australian sky

Union Jack   Aboriginal people

Blue colour in the T.S.S flag   Flag colours

TASK 3

Traditional food

Read and watch the following texts and videos:

Australia doesn't have any traditional dishes like Spain, Italy or France but they have typical Australian food such as for example Chicken Parmigiana, Barramundi, Meat Pies, Grilled Kangaroo, Barbecue Snags, Lamington or Pavlova.

https://amberstudent.com/blog/post/top-traditional-foods-in-australia

Kangaroo is considered one of the healthiest meat in Australia. It contains no fat at all and it is also rich in iron that's why more and more people who want to be healthy eat this meat. Kangaroo meat is usually grilled and served with vegetables such as potatoes and onions.

https://www.youtube.com/watch?v=jQV_mBnq6JI

Barramundi in Aboriginal Australian language means "big river fish" and it is considered a traditional fish. It can be fried or grilled and served with vegetables.

https://www.youtube.com/watch?v=oZtSsMOVNPU

Lamington is an australian traditional cake which
is made in squares and is covered by chocolate
and then by dried coconut.

https://www.youtube.com/watch?v=CbHWqzw4Qxg

Pavlova is a delicious cake topped with whipped cream and fruits. It is common for birthdays and also on important celebrations

https://www.youtube.com/watch?v=SjskNTkF9MM

TASK 2

Say if these sentences are True or False and correct the false ones.

1. Chicken Parmigiana is usually served with vegetables

....

2. Barramundi is an Australian dish

....

3. Pavlova is made of sponge cake, chocolate and coconut

....

4. Barbecue Snags are Australian sausages made of beef and pork meat

....

5. Meat Pies contain usually chicken meat and
    vegetables

    ....

6. Kangaroo meat contains a lot of fat

    ....

🌹 SAINT VALENTINE'S DAY 🌷

TASK 1

Read about Saint Valentine:

Saint Valentine is celebrated 14th February all over the world and it is the patron saint of lovers.

People express their love by sending cards, letters and different kinds of presents not only to their boyfriends, girlfriends, husbands or wifes but also to relatives or other people they love.

The first version of this festivity can be found back in time in Rome with the festival of Lupercalia that became the celebration of fertility at the beginning of Spring. This festivity was very popular and Constantine tried to eliminate it as he did with many other pagan activities. Finally, in the 5th Century Pope

Galasius changed the pagan Lupercalia for the Christian martyred bishop Valentine.

But, who was Saint Valentine? Saint Valentine was a Catholic priest who lived in the third Century in Rome. He refused to obey the Emperor by marrying young catholic soldiers in secret so they were not so ready to go to war. For this reason Saint Valentine was finally martyred and executed.

But it was no until the Middle Ages and the courtly love that Saint Valentine was connected to romantic love. In the 18th century people started giving small presents to their lovers and in the 19th century sending greeting cards became popular together with the symbols of the heart and Cupid. Today red roses, chocolates, greeting cards, cakes and cupcakes in the shape of a heart ..... are very popular.

TASK 2

Watch this video about how to prepare a
cupcake with a heart inside:

https://www.youtube.com/watch?v=VR8qFN5xVc
Y&list=PLcpoB2VESJmc1EnQeeWMe_s84gEZelx
BW&index=4

Name 5 of the ingredients you can use for this
recipe

    1. ………………………….
    2. ………………………….
    3. ………………………….
    4. ………………………….
    5. ………………………….

TASK 3

And what about Saint Valentine's drinks?

Lovebug cocktail

https://www.youtube.com/watch?v=yRJ6L1LedVg

Love potion

https://www.youtube.com/watch?v=IZuSrdSsrbY

Now, create your own cocktail and give it a name

....

....

....

....

....

TASK 4

Watch this TikTok of a Valentine's Day inspired Eton Mess. 💗

https://vm.tiktok.com/ZGebCHFLF/

What would you make for Valentine's Day? Attach a video to Google Classroom explaining the details.

....

....

SAINT DAVID

PATRON SAINT OF WALES

TASK 1

How much do you know about Saint David?

Tick the sentences you think are right

- He was a Celtic monk in the 6th century.
- Tradition says he was born during a storm.
- He expanded Christianity among the Celts.
- The rose is the national flower of Wales.
- He was a strict vegetarian.
- Shakespeare perpetuated St David's emblem.
- St David's Cathedral is a place of pilgrimage.
- No miracles are associated with him.
- There are just a few churches named after him.
- St David's Day is celebrated 1st March.

TASK 2

Check your answers in Task 1 by reading this text:

David was the son of the Celtic leader Sant and Non and tradition says he was born during a storm in the 6th century.

David became a Christian priest and years later he lived on an island for a long time being vegetarian and studying the Bible. When he left the island he founded a monastery in southern Wales and expanded Christianity among the Celts. It is said he performed several miracles and nowadays there are many churches and a Cathedral, a place of pilgrimage, named after him.

Saint David was canonised in the 12th century and later he became the national patron saint of Wales. For many centuries 1st March has been the national festival and it is celebrated with parades and parties.

According to a legend, St David recommended the Welsh soldiers to wear a leek on their helmets to be different from the Saxon soldiers invaders. From then on the leek is part of the Welsh soldiers uniforms. On the 1st March people celebrate St. David wearing a daffodil, national flower, or a leek, St. David symbol.

TASK 3

There are many symbols of Welsh food such as leek, potato and bacon soup, Cawl Cennin in Welsh, rarebit, Glamorgan sausage, laverbread or the famous Welsh cakes.

Leek, potato and bacon soup recipe:

Ingredients:

4 medium leeks

3 or 4 white potatoes

3 tbsp butter

4 cups vegetable or chicken stock

1 cup cream

250 grams bacon

Pinch black pepper

Instructions:

1- Sauté the chopped leeks and the bacon in butter.

2- Add the other ingredients except the cream and boil for 30 minutes.

3- Pureé with a food processor.

4- Pour back in the pan and add the cream.

5- Serve.

TASK 4

Welsh cakes recipe:

Watch the video and make a list of the ingredients to prepare them. 🥧

https://www.bbcgoodfood.com/recipes/welsh-cakes

…………………………………………

…………………………………………

…………………………………………

…………………………………………

…………………………………………

SAINT PATRICK

PATRON SAINT OF IRELAND

TASK 1

Read the text:

Saint Patrick's Day is celebrated March 17th, the feast day of St. Patrick, patron saint of Ireland. It has also become a celebration of Irish culture around the world.

But, who was Saint Patrick?

At the end of the fourth century in a Britain occupied by the Romans, Padráig was born in a family of priests. When he was sixteen pirates kidnapped him and he escaped after six years working as a shepherd. When he was back to Britain and his family, he decided to study to become first a priest and then a bishop. He became Patrick and worked for around 40 years in Ireland converting people to Christianity. Legend says he drove snakes out of the island.

What food is eaten on St. Patrick's day in Ireland?   Irish stew is one of the most popular dishes in Ireland. Other popular dishes are Corned beef and cabbage, Irish soda bread, fried cabbage, Colcannon (Irish mashed potatoes) and Irish apple tart.

TASK 2

Watch the video and answer the questions.

https://www.youtube.com/watch?v=8vUIYSDss9c

1. What was the colour originally associated with St. Patrick?

    ....

2. Why is it so popular to wear and use green?

    ....

3. Name three of the countries where people celebrate St. Patrick's Day

    ....

4. What is Ireland's nickname?

    ....

5. What two things are very commonly eaten on this feast?

....

....

TASK 3

Watch the video to know how to prepare Irish stew

https://www.youtube.com/watch?v=TYwv4ACc4iA&t=10s

Do you have any similar recipes in your country?
Name and find similarities and differences.

....

....

....

Do you celebrate Saint Patrick's Day in your
region?

....

....

....

TASK 4

Watch the video about how to prepare corned beef and cabbage.

https://www.youtube.com/watch?v=6GCtWGZubDc

Name the four main ingredients:

1. ………………………………………….
2. ………………………………………….
3. ………………………………………….
4. ………………………………………….

...And four preparation verbs:

1. ....

2. ....

3. ....

4. ....

TASK 1

Read the text:

Shrove Tuesday is the day before Lent which starts with Ash Wednesday and takes place 40 days before Easter. It is celebrated in the United Kingdom, Ireland, Canada and Australia.

Shrove comes from the word shrive that means to confess and be absolved so this day it is tradition for Christians to clean their soul through confession.

And, why Pancake Day or Pancake Tuesday? Because it is the last opportunity to eat all these delicious things before the 40 days of fasting and housewives used the remaining of all these "forbidden" ingredients such as milk, eggs or sugar before the beginning of Lent to make pancakes.

Pancake races are very popular in Britain. Tradition says that in 1445 a woman was preparing pancakes when the bells for church started to ring so she ran to the church with her apron and the frying pan with the pancake. This took place in Olney in Buckinghamshire and now this festival is famous all over the world.

TASK 2

To know more about Pancake Races watch these videos:

https://www.youtube.com/watch?v=wH3zVhmMIYk

https://www.youtube.com/watch?v=8yC_Of1DUes

TASK 3

Watch the video about how to prepare pancakes
and then make a list with the ingredients and the
quantities.

https://www.youtube.com/watch?v=MwN5m9ZBq
RI

Ingredients:

....

....

....

....

TASK 4

Watch this TikTok:

https://vm.tiktok.com/ZGebCwvCS/

Do you like this recipe? Why/why not?

....

Design your own pancake recipe for a specific occasion or festivity of your choice. Make a video presentation to attach as a task on Google Classroom. You will need to make it at home and explain why you made what you made and how to prepare it.

💗 MOTHERING SUNDAY 💁

TASK 1

Read the text:

Mother's day, also called Mothering Sunday, is celebrated all over the world, but not at the same time of the year. In the UK it is celebrated on the fourth Sunday of Lent. In America on the second Sunday of May.

Children give gifts and cards as a way to show their love to their mothers on Mothering Sunday. Sometimes children also show their gratitude with acts of kindness such as preparing a lovely breakfast and taking it to her bedroom or taking her out for lunch.

There is a typical dessert for this occasion called Simnel which is also very typical for Easter. It is made of dried fruits, orange flavoured liqueur, butter, ginger, caster sugar, icing sugar, eggs, flour and nutmeg. The cake is topped with 11 balls of marzipan which is made of almonds, egg whites and sugar and then baked. But why 11 balls? The 11 balls represent the apostles (all but Judas).

TASK 2

Watch the video and answer the questions:

https://www.youtube.com/watch?v=zVMQuSgNSm8

1- How many of the ingredients mentioned in the video are dairy products? ....

2- Name them ....

3- Are there any spices in the recipe? ....

4- Which ones? ....

5- What ingredients have animal origin?................

....

TASK 3

Watch these TikToks:

https://vm.tiktok.com/ZGebC4PSr/

https://vm.tiktok.com/ZGebCpm9R/

Make your own Mother's Day recipe. Make a Canva poster with photos and the main instructions to make it. Attach it to Google Classroom.

🐰 EASTER 🐰

TASK 1

Read the text and underline each one of the festivities:

Easter is the period of Jesus Christ's last days before his death.

It starts with Shrove Tuesday, also called Pancake Day (47 days before Easter Sunday). The following day is Ash Wednesday, which is the beginning of Lent.

On Palm Sunday Christians celebrate that Jesus arrives in Jerusalem and it is seven days before Easter Sunday.

Holy Thursday is the celebration of Jesus' Last Supper just before Holy Friday or Good Friday, the day Jesus died on the cross. This is followed by Holy Saturday; the end of Lent and the day Jesus is on the grave.

Finally, Easter Sunday is the day Jesus Christ came from the dead. It is a day to go to Church and sing. Many families go together for a special lunch which consists of roast lamb with mint sauce and vegetables followed by a Simnel cake. Family and friends get together to receive and give Easter eggs. Children go egg hunting, collecting the easter eggs which were hidden during the previous night.

TASK 2

Watch the video and answer the questions:

https://www.youtube.com/watch?v=pqod8RVRl50

What pieces of information are in the video and not in the text? Name three

....

....

....

What are hot cross buns?

....

....

....

TASK 3

Watch this TikTok:

https://vm.tiktok.com/ZGebC9P9M/

Make your own Easter-inspired cookie. Make a batch and show everyone in class what you made. Be ready to explain how you did it and why.

APRIL FOOL'S DAY

TASK 1

Read the text:

April Fool's Day is celebrated on 1 April around the world. People play practical jokes on this day and have fun trying to convince other people about things that are not true. You should only play jokes and tricks before noon because after this time it is considered very bad luck.

There are three different types of tricks: hoaxes, fool's errands and practical jokes. Hoaxes are intentional efforts to trick an audience and make it believe that something is real (but it is not). Fool's errands is to send someone to get an item that doesn't exist. Practical jokes are tricks to make someone appear foolish to enjoy others.

TASK 2

To know more about the history of April Fool's watch the following video:

https://www.youtube.com/watch?v=BpQzjef-gxw

TASK 3

Watch these two videos about some of the most famous jokes and answer the following questions:

https://www.youtube.com/watch?v=tVo_wkxH9dU

https://www.youtube.com/watch?v=H_t3Cjc6T_Q

1- What kind of trick can you see in the videos?

....

2- Do you think people thought they were real at the time?

....

3- If you make someone do something to others, is this a practical joke or a fool's errand?

....

4- And if you send someone to "hunt" a haggis in Scotland?

....

5- Can you think of any practical joke you've ever made on December 28th?

....

TASK 4

Watch this TikTok:

https://vm.tiktok.com/ZGebCvTfE/

What recipe would you make at home for your siblings, cousins or children?

....

Make a digital presentation and be ready to explain it to everyone in class.

🐎SAINT GEORGE'S DAY🐎

TASK 1

Read the text

St George was an officer in the Roman army. He protested against the Romans' torture of Christians. Roman emperor Diocletian ordered his death and that's how he became a Christian martyr.

St George represents the courage to face adversity to defend the innocent. The triumph of good over evil, through courage.

King Edward III, who reigned from 1327 to 1377 chose St George as England's patron saint. It is 23rd April, the day for a red rose but English people do not celebrate it.

The flag of England has a red cross in a white background for St. George and this emblem was adopted by King Richard, The Lion heart, in the 12th century.

TASK 2

Watch the video and answer the questions.

https://www.english-heritage.org.uk/visit/whats-on/st-georges-day/9-things-you-didnt-know-about-st-george/

1- What is the most popular story about St. George?

....

2- What does the dragon symbolise?

....

3- Do you find any similarity between St. George's dragon and St. Patrick's snake?

....

4- What did the dragon represent in the Middle Ages?

....

TASK 3

Circle the one related with St. George

Snake................Duck..............Dragon

England..........Scotland.......Ireland

Poppy................Rose..............Daffodil

Red..................Pink................Yellow

TASK 4

If you have arrived here you are ready to visit Britain and also to enjoy and prepare most of their popular dishes.

Watch this last video and enjoy... 

https://www.youtube.com/watch?v=eS5DPDojmk

Accessed links:

1. YouTube:

https://www.youtube.com/watch?v=_YgfYwaqZPy

https://www.youtube.com/watch?v=L7hHL33lQ0I

https://www.youtube.com/watch?v=YIqS6blTTwk

https://www.youtube.com/watch?v=8nngt2XvvHM

https://www.youtube.com/watch?v=fhgoB3qA_qk

https://www.youtube.com/watch?v=zWaGYgcFYu0

https://www.youtube.com/watch?v=DKblUst5sd0

https://www.youtube.com/watch?v=z_zMmEYGj54

https://www.youtube.com/watch?v=XO5DF8soxwM

https://www.youtube.com/watch?v=3XOKmaElzqw

https://www.youtube.com/watch?v=WDA60XAW7yo

https://www.youtube.com/watch?v=jQV_mBnq6JI

https://www.youtube.com/watch?v=oZtSsM0VNPU

https://www.youtube.com/watch?v=CbHWqzw4Qxg

https://www.youtube.com/watch?v=SjskNTkF9MM

https://www.youtube.com/watch?v=VR8qFN5xVcY&list=PLcpoB2VESJmc1EnQeeWMe_s84gEZelxBW&index=4

https://www.youtube.com/watch?v=yRJ6L1LedVg

https://www.youtube.com/watch?v=IZuSrdSsrbY

https://www.youtube.com/watch?v=8vUIYSDss9c

https://www.youtube.com/watch?v=TYwv4ACc4iA&t=10s

https://www.youtube.com/watch?v=6GCtWGZubDc

https://www.youtube.com/watch?v=zVMQuSgNSm8

https://www.youtube.com/watch?v=wH3zVhmMIYk

https://www.youtube.com/watch?v=8yC_Of1DUe
s

https://www.youtube.com/watch?v=MwN5m9ZBq
RI

https://www.youtube.com/watch?v=pqod8RVRl50

https://www.youtube.com/watch?v=BpQzjef-
gxw

https://www.youtube.com/watch?v=tVo_wkxH9d
U

https://www.youtube.com/watch?v=H_t3Cjc6T_
Q

https://www.youtube.com/watch?v=eS5DPDojmk

2. BBC:

https://www.bbcgoodfood.com/recipes/pumpkin-
pie

https://www.bbcgoodfood.com/recipes/pumpkin-
soup

https://www.bbcgoodfood.com/recipes/clootie-dumpling

https://www.bbcgoodfood.com/recipes/welsh-cakes

https://www.bbcgoodfood.com/recipes/simnel-cake

https://www.bbc.com/news/uk-england-beds-bucks-herts-64647048

https://www.bbc.co.uk/food/recipes/how_to_make_pancakes_02824

https://www.bbc.co.uk/newsround/65097329

3. Wikipedia:

https://en.wikipedia.org/wiki/Pumpkin_bread#:~:text=Pumpkin%20bread%20is%20a%20type,Pumpkin%20walnut%20bread

4. TikTok:

https://www.tiktok.com/@c4tluvr666/video/7279552380545355051?_r=1&_t=8gkxIJ7q5VR

https://www.tiktok.com/@c4tluvr666/video/713
5229252051602734?_r=1&_t=8gkxPQUxZfV

https://vm.tiktok.com/ZGebCvMJ7/

https://vm.tiktok.com/ZGebC7xhE/

https://vm.tiktok.com/ZGebCXheD/

https://vm.tiktok.com/ZGebCHFLF/

https://vm.tiktok.com/ZGebCwvCS/

https://vm.tiktok.com/ZGebC4PSr/

https://vm.tiktok.com/ZGebCpm9R/

https://vm.tiktok.com/ZGebC9P9M/

https://vm.tiktok.com/ZGebCvTfE/

5. Poetry Foundation:

https://www.poetryfoundation.org/poems/47380
/in-flanders-fields

6. Blogs:

https://amberstudent.com/blog/post/top-traditional-foods-in-australia

7. Other sites:

https://www.theedkins.co.uk/jo/maps/uktowns.htm

https://www.twinkl.es/teaching-wiki/3-flags-of-australia#:~:text=The%203%20flags%20of%20Australia%20include%20the%20Australian%20National%20Flag,been%20in%20use%20since%201901

https://www.mashed.com/811166/the-untold-truth-of-haggis/

https://www.etsy.com/listing/730950508/australian-food-watercolor-illustrations

https://www.sbs.com.au/food/recipe/kangaroo-with-red-wine-sauce-and-wild-rosella/snaxb0z4i

https://recipes.net/articles/what-is-barramundi/

https://www.thespruceeats.com/lamington-cake-recipe-256086

https://www.justapinch.com/recipes/dessert/other-dessert/australian-pavlova.html

https://www.history.com/news/is-st-patricks-day-celebrated-in-ireland

https://www.simplyrecipes.com/recipes/irish_beef_stew/

https://www.allrecipes.com/recipe/16310/corned-beef-and-cabbage-i/

https://www.english-heritage.org.uk/visit/whats-on/st-georges-day/9-things-you-didnt-know-about-st-george/